CRICKETS AND GRASSHOPPERS

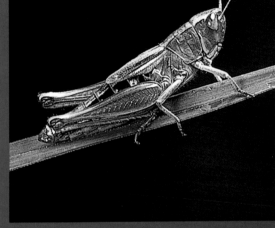

A TRUE BOOK®

by

Ann O. Squire

Children's Press®
A Division of Scholastic Inc.

New York Toronto London Auckland Sydney
Mexico City New Delhi Hong Kong
Danbury, Connecticut

Close-up
of a horned
katydid

Reading Consultant
Nanci R. Vargus, Ed.D.
Assistant Professor
Literacy Education
University of Indianapolis
Indianapolis, IN

Content Consultant
Jeff Hahn
Department of Entomology
University of Minnesota

Dedication:
For Emma and Evan

The photo on the cover shows
a mature grasshopper. The
photo on the title page shows
a grasshopper perched on a
blade of grass.

Library of Congress Cataloging-in-Publication Data

Squire, Ann.
   Crickets and Grasshoppers / by Ann O. Squire
      p. cm. — (True books)
   Includes bibliographical references and index (p.).
   ISBN 0-516-22657-6 (lib. bdg.)   0-516-29357-5 (pbk.)
   Orthoptera—Juvenile literature. [1. Crickets 2. Grasshoppers.] I. Title.
II. True book.
QL506.S65 2003
595.7'26—dc21   2002005882

1 2 3 4 5 6 7 8 9 10 R 12 11 10 09 08 07 06 05 04 03

Contents

Crickets (right) and grasshoppers (below) are well known for both their singing and jumping abilities.

Amazing Orthopterans

Can you name an animal that is as well known for its singing ability as it is for its high jump? Kangaroos are great leapers, but they don't sing. Whales sing complex songs to one another, but they certainly can't jump. Crickets and grasshoppers are experts at both. These insects, along with katydids and locusts, belong to the animal order **Orthoptera**, which comes from the Greek words *orthos* (straight) and *pteron* (wing). So it's not surprising to find that most crickets and grasshoppers have long, straight wings. Orthopterans also have oversized, muscular legs that enable them to jump incredible distances. If you could jump as high and as far as a grasshopper can for its size, you would be able to leap 300 feet (91 meters) in the air or travel 500 feet (152 m) down the street in a single hop.

Crickets and grasshoppers are also known for their loud songs, which fill the air on summer nights. But chirping orthopterans aren't really singing. They make their distinctive sounds by rubbing their wings together, or by

Crickets rub their legs against each other, or against one of their wings, to make noise.

scraping a hind leg against one wing—an activity called **stridulation**.

All orthopterans have mouthparts that are special-ized for chewing. Most species eat leaves, grasses, and other plant parts. Some, like the desert locust, are major plant pests. Swarms of these hungry insects have been known to eat 3,000 tons (6 million pounds or 2 million kilograms) of green

Orthopterans, such as this grasshopper, have huge appetites.

plants in a single day. That's about the same weight as five hundred full-grown African elephants.

Champion Chewers

Although there are more than one million zebras, gazelles, and other grazing animals on Africa's Serengeti Plain, grasshoppers eat more grass than all the larger animals put together.

Cricket or Grasshopper?

Hopping and singing are two activities all orthopterans have in common. There are some big differences among species as well. There are five distinct groups (called families) within the **order** Orthoptera. One family includes the hungry grasshoppers and locusts we

Short-horned grasshoppers get their name from their small antennae.

met in the first chapter. These insects can be recognized by their short antennae. In fact, members of this group are usually called short-horned grasshoppers. They produce sounds by rubbing a row of pegs on their hind legs against their forewings. They "hear" through a membrane called a tympanum, which is located on the abdomen. Short-horned grasshoppers and locusts are usually **diurnal** (active during the day).

You might be wondering what is making all that noise at night because grasshoppers and locusts are diurnal. There are several possibilities. It could

A tree cricket's chirps depend on the temperature.

be an insect in the cricket
family, a group whose members
are usually dull in color and
have very long antennae.

This katydid looks very much like a tree leaf.

Crickets spend their days hiding in the grass or under stones or logs and come out to sing when night falls. It could be a species of tree cricket, a pale green or whitish insect whose chirping rate is related to temperature. The hotter the weather gets, the faster this little cricket chirps. Or the chirping could be a katydid, which is a slender, green insect that rests during the day, **camouflaged** on a leaf.

Katydids rub their wings together to make noise.

Crickets and katydids make sounds in a different way than do grasshoppers and locusts.

18

While grasshoppers and locusts rub their hind legs against their wings, crickets and katydids rub a scraper on one wing against a file on the other wing. Their hearing organs are in a different place, too. They are inside a slit on the front legs.

One of the most unusual orthopterans is in a family all its own. The mole cricket spends most of its time underground in a burrow that

A mole cricket lives underground.

it digs using its large, flattened forelegs. Males come to the surface at night to sing for a mate. So, while you may occasionally hear a mole cricket, you'll probably never see one.

Why Do They Sing?

Have you ever wondered why crickets and grasshoppers make so much noise? Like a roaring lion or a singing robin, a chirping grasshopper is sending a message to other members of its species. Since grasshoppers and crickets spend most of their time hidden in the grass or

Crickets and other orthopterans use sound to find each other.

under leaves, they rarely see one another. For these insects, sound is one of the easiest ways to stay in touch.

For locusts, which travel in huge swarms, chirping may help group members to stay together and head in the same direction. Male grasshoppers use song to stake out their territories and keep other males

Locusts use sound to help keep the members of a swarm together.

A grasshopper has a special call that helps it find other members of the same species.

away. By far, the most important use for orthopteran song is in mating.

In most cricket and grasshopper species, it is the males

who have the job of finding and attracting a mate. On warm evenings in late summer and early fall, the air is filled with mating chirps. Every species sings a different song, and females only respond to the songs of their own species. So, there is no chance of a male cricket mating with a female grasshopper, or vice versa.

When a female hears her species' mating chirp, she turns toward the sound, waving her

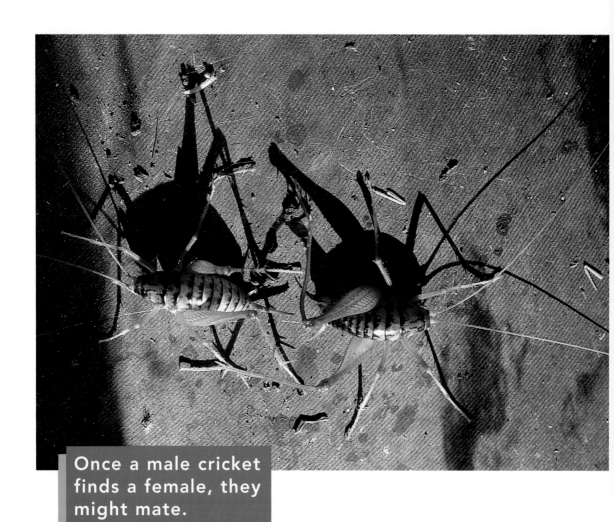

Once a male cricket finds a female, they might mate.

antennae about. In some
species, the female gives an
answering chirp, and both

male and female move toward each other. But in many species, the females cannot sing, so the male continues his song as the female finds him by moving closer to the sound. If all goes well, the two get together for mating.

Sometimes, however, a chirping male grasshopper is interrupted by a rival, who tries to convince the female to choose him instead. When this happens, the two males trade

Sometimes male grasshoppers compete to impress a female.

aggressive songs until one decides to move on. If the rivalry goes on for too long, the female sometimes leaves, deserting the males in the middle of their argument.

In crickets, this rivalry is even more intense. If a male cricket can't convince his competitor to leave by chirping at him, the next step is a wrestling match. The two opponents lock their mouthparts together and kick viciously with their hind legs. This sometimes results in the death of one of the insects. Cricket fighting was once a popular sport in China. Huge amounts of money were won and lost in tournaments.

An Orthopteran Grows Up

After mating, male and female orthopterans go their separate ways and, after a short time, the females are ready to lay their eggs. Female crickets and grasshoppers have a long, slender tube called an **ovipositor** at the end of the abdomen.

A female grasshopper sticks her
ovipositor in the ground to lay eggs.

Short-horned grasshoppers and locusts have ovipositors that are short and blunt, like a chisel. Long-horned grasshoppers, crickets, and katydids have long, curved, swordlike ovipositors. All ovipositors are used in the same way. First, the female makes a hole in the ground, using her ovipositor as a drill. Then she lays her eggs, which pass through the hollow tube and are pushed

deep into the soil. There they will be safe for the long, cold winter.

These grasshopper nymphs look like tiny adult grasshoppers.

When the eggs hatch in the spring, the tiny crickets and grasshoppers tunnel to the surface. At this stage of life, they are called **nymphs**. A nymph looks very much like an adult, except that it is smaller and has only tiny buds where its wings should be. As the nymph grows, its **exoskeleton** (the hard outer skin covering the insect's body) becomes tighter and tighter. Finally, the exoskeleton splits, and the growing grasshopper slides out, leaving the old skin behind. This process is called **molting**, and it will happen five or six times

A grasshopper crawls out of its skin and leaves it behind.

before the little nymph becomes a full-grown cricket or grasshopper.

With each molt, the little wing buds get larger. By the insect's final molt, the wings are fully developed, and ready to use for flying and singing.

A Tasty Treat?

Fried grasshoppers

You may think it's disgusting, but entomophagy (the eating of insects) is a common practice in some parts of the world. In Mexico, fried grasshoppers are very popular. You can buy them by the pound in village markets or in cans in the grocery store.

A woman sells fried grasshoppers in a Mexican market.

Escape Artists

Life holds many dangers for crickets and grasshoppers. Nymphs are especially vulnerable because they cannot yet fly. Even adult orthopterans are always in danger of becoming tasty snacks for a bird, snake, lizard, mouse, or even a spider.

A woodpecker caught a grasshopper for a tasty meal.

Fortunately, crickets and grasshoppers can escape from many of their enemies by leaping away. A few species, including the African "stinking grasshopper," fight back by discharging a bad-smelling liquid from glands on their bodies.

It is also possible to avoid danger by hiding in plain sight. As you can see from the photographs throughout this book, most orthopterans come in shades of green, black, or brown. These colors help them to hide from their enemies by blending in with their environments. Most crickets spend their days under logs or

This brown cricket (right) easily blends into the rain forest floor. It's hard to spot the mottled grasshopper among these stones (below).

among fallen leaves. Not surprisingly, these insects are usually dull brown in color.

This green leaf mimic katydid looks just like the leaves it sits next to.

Katydids, on the other hand, are not dull at all. A bright green katydid resting on a bright green leaf is very difficult to spot, and its long, leaf-shaped wings make this insect's camouflage even more effective. Grasshopper nymphs are almost identical in shape and color to the blades of grass they eat. So the next time you're outside on a summer afternoon, look around and see how many hidden orthopterans you can spot right in your own backyard.

To Find Out More

If you'd like to learn more about crickets and grasshoppers, check out these additional resources.

 **Books**

Johnson, Sylvia A. **Chirping Insects.** Lerner Publications, 1986.

Miller, Sara Swan. **Grasshoppers and Crickets of North America (Animals in Order**). Danbury, CT: Franklin Watts, 2002.

Pascoe, Elaine. **Crickets and Grasshoppers (Nature Close-Up).** Woodbridge, CT: Blackbirch Press, 1998. — Includes hands-on projects to help kids learn more about orthopterans.

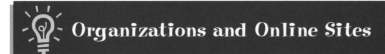

Organizations and Online Sites

Crickets and Grasshoppers

http://www.yahooligans. com/science_and_nature/liv- ing_things/animals/inverte- brates/arthropods/insects/ Crickets_and_Grasshoppers/

This site contains excellent photos of grasshoppers, crickets, katydids, and other insects, along with a basic introduction to a vari- ety of species.

Young Entomologists' Society, Inc.
6907 West Grand River Ave. Lansing, MI 48906

This organization provides outreach programs for young people interested in studying insects.

Important Words

camouflage devices that animals use to blend into their environments

diurnal active during daylight hours

exoskeleton the hard outer covering of an insect's body

molt to shed an old, outgrown skin

nymph immature form of an orthopteran

order a group of creatures within a class that shares certain characteristics

orthoptera the scientific order that includes crickets and grasshoppers

ovipositor a long tube at the end of a female orthopteran's abdomen that is used for digging a hole and laying eggs

stridulation making sounds by rubbing specialized body parts together

Index

Meet the Author

Ann O. Squire has a Ph.D. in animal behavior. Before becoming a writer, she spent several years studying African electric fish and the special signals they use to communicate

with each other. Dr. Squire is the author of many books on animals and natural science topics, including *Animal Homes*, *Animal Babies*, *Fossils*, and *Seashells*. She lives with her children, Emma and Evan, in Katonah, New York.

Photographs © 2003: Dembinsky Photo Assoc.: 13 (E.R. Degginger), 39 (Dan Dempster), 4 bottom (Skip Moody), 34 (Gail Nachel), 18 (Rod Planck); Dwight R. Kuhn Photography: cover, 4 top; Minden Pictures: 42 (Gerry Ellis), 16 (Frans Lanting); Peter Arnold Inc.: 2 (S.J. Krasemann), 28, 33 (Hans Pfletschinger), 41 bottom (Ed Reschke); Photo Researchers, NY: 1 (Stephen Dalton/NHPA), 36 (J.H. Robinson), 23 (Gianni Tortoli); Robert & Linda Mitchell: 8, 10, 11 top, 11 bottom, 15, 20, 22, 24, 31, 37 left, 37 right, 41 top; Visuals Unlimited/John Serrao: 26.